Air Fryer Plant Based Cookbook

40 Amazing And Tasty Recipes To Become A True Vegetarian Chef With The Air Fryer

Christopher Ramsay

TABLE OF CONTENTS

Air Fryer Green Meals Recipes

Orange Mango Salad

Preparation time: 5 minutes Cooking time: 8 minutes

Servings: 4

INGREDIENTS

- 1 cup mango, peeled and cubed 1 cup baby spinach

- 1 cup cherry tomatoes, halved

- 1 cup oranges, peeled and cut into segments 1

tablespoon olive oil

- 1 tablespoon balsamic vinegar 2 teaspoons orange

zest, grated A handful parsley, chopped

DIRECTIONS

1.   In the air fryer's pan, mix the mango with the

spinach and the other ingredients, toss and cook at

350 degrees F for 8 minutes.

2.   Divide into bowls and serve.

NUTRITION: Calories 151, Fat 6, Fiber 6, Carbs

11, Protein 5

Avocado Salad

Preparation time: 5 minutes Cooking time: 5 minutes

Servings: 4

INGREDIENTS

• red onion, sliced

• cups avocado, peeled, pitted and cubed 1 cup cherry

tomatoes, halved

• 2 tablespoons avocado oil Juice of 1 lime

• Salt and black pepper to the taste 1 cup walnuts,

chopped

• 1 tablespoon chives, chopped

DIRECTIONS

In your air fryer, mix the avocado with the tomatoes and the other ingredients, toss, cook at 400 degrees F for 5 minutes, divide into bowls and serve.

NUTRITION: Calories 151, Fat 4, Fiber 6,

Carbs 9,

Protein 4

Tomato and Shrimp Salad

Preparation time: 6 minutes Cooking time: 6

minutes Servings: 4

INGREDIENTS

- 1 pound cherry tomatoes, halved

- ½ pound shrimp, peeled and deveined Juice of 1 lime

- 1 cup baby kale

- 2 green onions, chopped 2 tomatoes, cubed

- jalapeno pepper, chopped 1 tablespoon olive oil

- teaspoons chili powder

- Salt and black pepper to the taste

DIRECTIONS

1.   In a pan that fits your air fryer, mix the

tomatoes with the shrimp, oil and the other

ingredients, toss, introduce the pan in the fryer and cook at 400 degrees F for 6 minutes.

2.   Divide the mix into bowls and serve.

NUTRITION: Calories 200, Fat 4, Fiber 7, Carbs 12, Protein 6

Bell Peppers Salad

Preparation time: 10 minutes Cooking time: 15 minutes Servings: 4

INGREDIENTS

- 2 red bell peppers, cut into strips
- 2 green bell peppers, cut into strips 2 orange bell peppers, cut into strips 1 cup cherry tomatoes, halved
- cup baby spinach Juice of 1 lime
- tablespoons olive oil
- Salt and black pepper to the taste

DIRECTIONS

1.   In a pan that fits your air fryer, mix the peppers with the tomatoes and the other ingredients, toss,

introduce the pan in the fryer and cook at 360 degrees F for 15 minutes.

2.	Divide into bowls and serve.

NUTRITION: Calories 161, Fat 7, Fiber 6, Carbs 12, Protein 7

Garlic Carrots and Spinach Salad

Preparation time: 10 minutes Cooking time: 15 minutes Servings: 4

INGREDIENTS

- 1 pound baby carrots, peeled and sliced 1 cup baby spinach
- 1 cup corn
- Juice of ½ lemon
- 1 tablespoon olive oil 6 garlic cloves, minced
- 1 tablespoon balsamic vinegar Salt and black pepper to the taste

DIRECTIONS

1.   In the air fryer's pan, mix the carrots with the spinach and the other ingredients, toss and cook at 380 degrees F for 15 minutes.

2.   Divide into bowls and serve.

Sprouts and Pomegranate Mix

Preparation time: 5 minutes Cooking time: 10

minutes Servings: 4

INGREDIENTS

- 1 pound Brussels sprouts, trimmed and halved

- 1 cup pomegranate seeds 1 cup baby spinach

- tablespoon avocado oil

- tablespoons balsamic vinegar 1 teaspoon chili powder

- Salt and black pepper to the taste

DIRECTIONS

1.   In the air fryer's pan, mix the sprouts with the

pomegranate seeds and the other ingredients, toss and

cook at 380 degrees F for 10 minutes.

2.   Divide into bowls and serve. **NUTRITION:**

Calories 141, Fat 3, Fiber 4, Carbs

11, Protein 4

Cauliflower and Pomegranate Mix

Preparation time: 6 minutes Cooking time: 12 minutes

Servings: 4

INGREDIENTS

- 1 pound cauliflower florets 1 cup pomegranate seeds 1 tablespoon lime juice

- 1 tablespoon orange juice 1 tablespoon olive oil

- Salt and black pepper to the taste 2 tablespoons chives, chopped

DIRECTIONS

1.   In your air fryer's pan, mix the cauliflower with the pomegranate seeds and the other ingredients, toss,

and cook at 400 degrees F for 12 minutes.

2.   Divide into bowls and serve.

NUTRITION: Calories 200, Fat 7, Fiber 5, Carbs 17, Protein 7

Potato Salad

Preparation time: 4 minutes Cooking time: 25 minutes Servings: 4

INGREDIENTS

- 1 pound sweet potatoes, peeled and cut into wedges
- 1 cup baby spinach
- 1 cup cherry tomatoes, halved
- 1 cup black olives, pitted and halved 1 tablespoon olive oil
- 1 teaspoon hot paprika 1 tablespoon lime juice
- Salt and black pepper to the taste

DIRECTIONS

1.   In your air fryer, combine the potatoes with the spinach and the other ingredients, toss and cook at

400 degrees F for 25 minutes.

2.   Divide into bowls and serve hot.

NUTRITION: Calories 151, Fat 4, Fiber 7, Carbs

12, Protein 6

Baby Potatoes Mix

Preparation time: 10 minutes Cooking time: 20

minutes Servings: 4

INGREDIENTS

• 1 pound baby potatoes, peeled and halved 1 cup green

beans, trimmed and halved

• cup corn

• tablespoons avocado oil Juice of 1 lime

• Salt and black pepper to the taste 3 garlic cloves,

minced

• ½ teaspoon rosemary, dried 1 teaspoon turmeric

powder 1 tablespoon dill, chopped

DIRECTIONS

1.   In the air fryer's pan, mix the potatoes with the

green beans and the other ingredients, toss and cook

at 400 degrees F for 20 minutes.

2. Divide between plates and serve.

NUTRITION: Calories 171, Fat 5, Fiber 6, Carbs 15, Protein 8

Cabbage Salad

Preparation time: 10 minutes Cooking time: 15

minutes Servings: 4

INGREDIENTS

- 1 pound red cabbage, shredded 1 red onion, sliced

- 1 cup carrots, peeled and shredded Juice of 1 lime

- tablespoon olive oil

- ¼ teaspoon sweet paprika

- Salt and black pepper to the taste 1 tablespoon dill,

chopped

DIRECTIONS

1.   In a pan that fits your air fryer, mix the

cabbage with the onion and the other ingredients ,

toss, introduce the pan in the fryer and cook at 400

degrees F for 15 minutes.

2.   Divide into bowls and serve.

NUTRITION: Calories 154, Fat 4, Fiber 4, Carbs

12, Protein 5

Cabbage and Pomegranate Mix

Preparation time: 10 minutes Cooking time: 12

minutes Servings: 4

INGREDIENTS

- 1 pound green cabbage, shredded

- ¼ cup butter, melted

- 1 cup pomegranate seeds

- 1 tablespoon chives, chopped

- A pinch of salt and black pepper 1 tablespoon sweet

paprika

- 1 tablespoon dill, chopped

DIRECTIONS

1.   In a pan that fits your air fryer, mix the cabbage

with the butter and the other ingredients, toss,

introduce the pan in the fryer and cook at 380 degrees F for 12 minutes.

2.   Divide everything into bowls and serve.

NUTRITION: Calories 181, Fat 4, Fiber 6, Carbs 15, Protein 5

Kale Salad

Preparation time: 4 minutes Cooking time: 15 minutes

Servings: 4

INGREDIENTS

- 1 pound baby kale 1 cup corn

- 1 cup cherry tomatoes, halved 1 tablespoon olive oil

- Juice of 1 lime

- Salt and black pepper to the taste

- ½ cup spring onions, chopped

DIRECTIONS

1. In a pan that fits your air fryer, mix the kale with the corn and the other ingredients, toss, introduce the pan in the fryer and cook at 350 degrees F for 15 minutes.

2. Divide the salad into bowls and serve.

NUTRITION: Calories 151, Fat 4, Fiber 5, Carbs 15, Protein 6

Spicy Green Beans Mix

Preparation time: 5 minutes Cooking time: 15 minutes

Servings: 4

INGREDIENTS

- 1 pound green beans, trimmed and halved 2 red chilies, minced
- 1 tablespoon lemon juice 1 tablespoon olive oil
- 1 teaspoon hot paprika
- A pinch of salt and black pepper
- tablespoons chives, chopped

DIRECTIONS

1.   In a pan that fits your air fryer, mix the green beans with the chilies and the other ingredients, toss, introduce in the fryer and cook at 320 degrees F for 15

minutes.

2.   Divide between plates and serve right away.

NUTRITION: Calories 124, Fat 6, Fiber 6, Carbs

16, Protein 7

Roast Celeriac

Preparation time: 10 minutes Cooking time: 15 minutes Servings: 4

INGREDIENTS

- 2 cups celeriac, peeled and roughly cubed 2 tablespoons olive oil
- Juice of 1 lime
- A pinch of salt and black pepper
- ½ tablespoon chives, chopped

DIRECTIONS

1. In the air fryer, combine the celeriac with the oil and the other ingredients, toss and cook at 380 degrees F for 15 minutes.

2. Divide between plates and serve.

NUTRITION: Calories 124, Fat 1, Fiber 4, Carbs 6, Protein 6

Maple Corn

Preparation time: 5 minutes Cooking time: 15 minutes Servings: 4

INGREDIENTS

- 2 cups corn

- 1 tablespoon avocado oil Juice of 1 lime

- 1 tablespoon maple syrup

- Salt and black pepper to the taste

- 1 tablespoon chives, chopped

DIRECTIONS

1.   In the air fryer, combine the corn with the oil and the other ingredients, toss and cook at 390 degrees F for 15 minutes.

2.   Divide the mix between plates and serve.

NUTRITION: Calories 100, Fat 2, Fiber 3, Carbs 8, Protein 3

Dill Mango and Corn

Preparation time: 5 minutes Cooking time: 12 minutes

Servings: 4

INGREDIENTS

- 2 cups corn

- 1 cup mango, peeled and cubed

- 1 cup baby spinach

- 1 tablespoon olive oil Juice of 1 lime

- Salt and black pepper to the taste

- 2 tablespoon dill, chopped

DIRECTIONS

1.   In your air fryer, combine the corn with the mango and the other ingredients, toss and cook at 390 degrees F for 12 minutes.

2.   Divide the mix into bowls and serve.

NUTRITION: Calories 100, Fat 2, Fiber 5, Carbs 9, Protein 6

Spring Onions and Pasta

Preparation time: 10 minutes Cooking time: 15 minutes

Servings: 4

INGREDIENTS

• 2 tablespoons butter, melted 2 cups small pasta

• ½ cup spring onions, chopped 1 cup heavy cream

• 1 cup chicken stock

• Salt and black pepper to the taste 1 tablespoon parmesan, grated

• 1 tablespoon chives, chopped

DIRECTIONS

1.   Grease A Baking Dish That Fits Your Air Fryer With The Butter, Combine All The Ingredients Inside, Introduce The Dish In The Fryer And Cook At 390 Degrees F For 15 Minutes.

2.   Divide Everything Between Plates And Serve.

NUTRITION: Calories 151, Fat 6, Fiber 5, Carbs 12, Protein 4

Mustard Greens and Spinach

Preparation time: 10 minutes Cooking time: 12 minutes Servings: 4

INGREDIENTS

- 1 pound mustard greens, torn

- ½ pound spinach, torn

- 1 cup cherry tomatoes, halved

- 1 cup black olives, pitted and halved 1 teaspoon sweet paprika

- A drizzle of olive oil

- Salt and black pepper to the taste

- ½ cup veggie stock

DIRECTIONS

1.	In a pan that fits your air fryer, mix the mustard greens with the spinach and the other ingredients, toss, introduce the pan in the fryer and cook at 300 degrees

F for 12 minutes.

2.   Divide everything between plates and serve.

NUTRITION: Calories 161, Fat 4, Fiber 5, Carbs

14, Protein 3

Balsamic Spinach

Preparation time: 10 minutes Cooking time: 12

minutes

Servings: 4

INGREDIENTS

• 1 pound spinach

• 2 tablespoons olive oil

• ½ cup chicken stock

• 1 teaspoon coriander, ground 1 teaspoon rosemary,

dried

• 1 cup cherry tomatoes, halved Salt and black pepper

to the taste 1 tablespoon balsamic vinegar

DIRECTIONS

1.   In a pan that fits your air fryer, mix the

spinach with the oil and the other ingredients, toss,

introduce in the fryer and cook at 260 degrees F for

12 minutes.

2.   Divide everything into bowls and serve.

NUTRITION: Calories 151, Fat 2, Fiber 4, Carbs

14, Protein 4

Endives and Pomegranate Mix

Preparation time: 10 minutes Cooking time: 12

minutes Servings: 4

INGREDIENTS

- 4 endives, trimmed and shredded 1 cup pomegranate

seeds

- 1 cup baby spinach

- Salt and black pepper to the taste

- 1 tablespoon lime juice 1 tablespoon olive

oil

- 1 teaspoon chili powder

DIRECTIONS

1. In air fryer, mix the endives with the pomegranate

seeds and the other ingredients, toss, cook at 360

degrees F for 12 minutes, divide between plates and

serve.

NUTRITION: Calories 100, Fat 3, Fiber 4,

Carbs 8,Protein 4

Nutmeg Endives

Preparation time: 10 minutes Cooking time: 12 minutes Servings: 4

INGREDIENTS

- 4 endives, trimmed and halved 1 teaspoon nutmeg, ground

- 1 teaspoon sweet paprika 2 tablespoons avocado oil Juice of 1 lime

- Salt and black pepper to the taste

DIRECTIONS

1.   Put the endives in your air fryer's basket, add the rest of the ingredients, toss and cook at 360 degrees F for 12 minutes.

2.   Divide the mix between plates and serve.

NUTRITION: Calories 151, Fat 6, Fiber 8, Carbs 14, Protein 6

Leeks and Grapes Mix

Preparation time: 5 minutes Cooking time: 15 minutes

Servings: 4

INGREDIENTS

• 4 leeks, sliced

• 1 cup grapes

• 1 tablespoon avocado oil Juice of 1 lime

• 1 avocado, peeled, pitted and cubed Salt and black

pepper to the taste

• 1 tablespoon chives, chopped

DIRECTIONS

1.   In the air fryer's pan, combine the leeks with the

grapes and the other ingredients, toss and cook at 360

degrees F for 15 minutes.

2.   Divide into bowls and serve.

NUTRITION: Calories 108, Fat 6, Fiber 1.7, Carbs

13.2, Protein 1.7

Rice, Mushrooms and Pomegranate Mix

Preparation time: 10 minutes Cooking time: 25 minutes Servings: 4

INGREDIENTS

- 1 cup white rice
- ½ cup pomegranate seeds
- cup white mushrooms, sliced 1 tablespoon olive oil
- cups chicken stock
- Salt and black pepper to the taste
- ½ teaspoon chili powder
- 1 tablespoon cilantro, chopped

DIRECTIONS

1.   In your air fryer's pan, combine the rice with the pomegranate seeds and the other ingredients, toss, and

cook at 360 degrees F for 25 minutes.

2.   Divide the mix between plates and serve.

NUTRITION: Calories 182, Fat 1.6, Fiber 2, Carbs

37.5, Protein 4.3

Sprouts and Leeks

Preparation time: 5 minutes Cooking time: 20 minutes Servings: 4

INGREDIENTS

- 1 pound Brussels sprouts, trimmed and halved
- 2 leeks, sliced
- ½ cup veggie stock
- 2 tablespoons chives, chopped 1 tablespoon avocado oil
- 1 teaspoon chili powder
- 1 teaspoon turmeric powder
- Salt and black pepper to the taste

DIRECTIONS

1. In the air fryer's pan, mix the sprouts with the leeks and the other ingredients, toss and cook everything for 20 minutes at 380 degrees F.

2.   Divide the mix between plates and serve.

NUTRITION: Calories 200, Fat 15.1, Fiber 5, Carbs 15.2, Protein 5.1

Green Beans and Avocado Mix

Preparation time: 10 minutes Cooking time: 20

minutes Servings: 4

INGREDIENTS

• 2 pounds green beans, trimmed and halved 1 cup

avocado, peeled, pitted and cubed

• 1 cup mango, peeled and cubed 1 tablespoon olive oil

• 1 teaspoon chili powder

• 1 tablespoon lemon zest, grated 1 tablespoon lemon

juice

• Salt and black pepper to the taste

DIRECTIONS

1.   In the air fryer's pan, combine the green beans

with the avocado and the other ingredients, toss and

cook at 360 degrees F for 20 minutes.

2.   Divide between plates and serve.

NUTRITION: Calories 108, Fat 4, Fiber 8, Carbs

17.4, Protein 4.4

Curry Green Beans

Preparation time: 5 minutes Cooking time: 20

minutes Servings: 4

INGREDIENTS

• 1 pound green beans, trimmed and halved 1

tablespoon green curry paste

• 1 tablespoons butter, melted 1 teaspoon curry powder

• ¼ cup veggie stock

• 1 teaspoon sweet paprika

• A pinch of salt and black pepper 1 tablespoon chives,

chopped

DIRECTIONS

1.   In your air fryer's pan, mix the green beans

with the curry paste and the other ingredients, toss and

cook at 360 degrees F for 20 minutes.

2.   Divide everything between plates and serve.

NUTRITION: Calories 194, Fat 4, Fiber 4, Carbs 8.4, Protein 7

Zucchini and Avocado Mix

Preparation time: 5 minutes Cooking time: 15 minutes

Servings: 4

INGREDIENTS

• 1 pound zucchinis, roughly cubed

• 1 cup avocado, peeled, pitted and cubed 1 tablespoon

olive oil

• Juice of 1 lime

• 1 teaspoon nutmeg, ground

• Salt and black pepper to the taste

• ½ teaspoon garlic powder

• 1 tablespoon chives, chopped

DIRECTIONS

1. In the air fryer's pan, mix the zucchinis with the avocado and the other ingredients, toss and cook at 360 degrees F for 15 minutes.

2. Divide between plates and serve.

NUTRITION: Calories 210, Fat 5, Fiber 7, Carbs 12, Protein 5

Spicy Tomatoes

Preparation time: 5 minutes Cooking time: 15 minutes

Servings: 4

INGREDIENTS

- 1 pound cherry tomatoes, halved 1 teaspoon chili

powder

- 1 teaspoon hot paprika
- 1 jalapenos, chopped Juice of 1 lime
- 2 tablespoon olive oil 2 garlic cloves, minced
- Salt and black pepper to the taste

DIRECTIONS

1.   In the air fryer's pan, combine the tomatoes

with the chili powder and the other ingredients, toss

and cook at 350 degrees F for 15 minutes.

2.   Divide between plates and serve.

NUTRITION: Calories 174, Fat 5, Fiber 7, Carbs

11, Protein 4

Tarragon Brussels Sprouts

Preparation time: 5 minutes Cooking time: 20 minutes Servings: 4

INGREDIENTS

- 2 pounds Brussels sprouts, trimmed and halved

- 1 teaspoon chili powder

- 1 teaspoon cumin, ground

- 1 tablespoon tarragon, chopped 2 tablespoons avocado oil

- 1 teaspoon sweet paprika

- Salt and black pepper to the taste 1 tablespoon dill, chopped

DIRECTIONS

1.   In the air fryer's basket, combine the sprouts

2.   with the chili powder and the other

ingredients, toss and cook at 360 degrees F for 20

minutes.

3.   Divide between plates and serve.

NUTRITION: Calories 214, Fat 5, Fiber 8, Carbs

12, Protein 5

Rosemary Eggplant

Preparation time: 5 minutes Cooking time: 20 minutes Servings: 4

INGREDIENTS

- 2 pounds eggplants, roughly cubed 1 tablespoon rosemary, chopped Juice of 1 lime
- 1 tablespoon olive oil
- 1 teaspoon cumin, ground
- Salt and black pepper to the taste 1 tablespoon cilantro, chopped

DIRECTIONS

1.	In the air fryer, combine the eggplants with the rosemary and the other ingredients, toss, and cook at 360 degrees F for 20 minutes.

2.   Divide the mix between plates and serve.

NUTRITION: Calories 182, Fat 6, Fiber 3, Carbs

11, Protein 5

Hot Fennel Mix

Preparation time: 5 minutes Cooking time: 20 minutes

Servings: 4

INGREDIENTS

- 1 fennel bulbs, sliced
- 1 teaspoon cumin, ground 1 tablespoon avocado oil 1 tablespoon orange juice
- 1 teaspoon smoked paprika 1 teaspoon

chili powder

- Salt and black pepper to the taste

DIRECTIONS

1.   In your air fryer, combine fennel with the cumin and the other ingredients, toss and cook at 360 degrees F for 20 minutes.

2.   Divide the mix between plates and serve.

Air Fryer Roasted Brussels Sprouts

Servings: 2

Cooking Time: 20 minutes

INGREDIENTS

- 1-pound Brussels sprouts 1 ½ tablespoons olive oil

- ½ teaspoon salt

- ½ teaspoon black pepper

DIRECTIONS

Preheat the air fryer at 3750F.

1.   Place the grill pan accessory in the air fryer.

2.   Put the Brussels sprouts in a mixing bowl and toss the remaining ingredients.

3.   Place the Brussels sprouts on the grill pan and cook for 20 minutes.

4. Give a good shake to cook the Brussels sprouts immediately.

NUTRITION: Calories: 189; Carbs: 20.7g; Protein: 7.7g; Fat: 10.8g

Air Fried Grilled Asparagus

Servings: 1

Cooking Time: 15 minutes

INGREDIENTS

• ½ bunch asparagus spears, trimmed Salt and pepper

to taste

• 1 tablespoon olive oil

DIRECTIONS

1.   Preheat the air fryer at 3750F.

2.   Place the grill pan accessory in the air fryer.

Season the asparagus with salt and pepper.

3.   Drizzle with oil.

4.   Place on the grill pan and cook for 15 minutes.

5.   Give the air fryer a good shake to cook evenly.

NUTRITION: Calories: 138; Carbs: 4.3g; Protein:

0.9g; Fat: 13.5g

Grilled Hasselback Potatoes

Servings: 1

Cooking Time: 25 minutes

INGREDIENTS

- 1 large potato

- 1 tablespoon butter

- ½ tablespoon oil

- Salt and pepper to taste

DIRECTIONS

1. Preheat the air fryer at 375OF.

2. Place the grill pan accessory in the air fryer.

3. Place the potato on a cutting board. Place

chopsticks on each side of the potato and slice until

where the cut marks are.

4. Brush potato with butter and oil. Season with salt and pepper to taste.

5. Place on the grill pan and cook for 20 to 25 minutes

NUTRITION: Calories: 464; Carbs: 68.7g; Protein: 8.7g; Fat: 18.6g

Air Fryer Roasted Vegetables

Servings: 4

Cooking Time: 15 minutes

INGREDIENTS

• 1 teaspoon olive oil

• 1 bunch asparagus spears, trimmed

• 1 yellow squash, seeded and cut in circles 1 zucchini, seeded and cut in circles

• 1 cup button mushrooms, quartered

• Salt and pepper to taste

• 1 teaspoon basil powder 1 teaspoon thyme

DIRECTIONS

1. Preheat the air fryer at 375OF.

2. Place the grill pan accessory in the air fryer.

3. Mix all vegetables in a bowl and toss to coat everything with the seasoning.

4.   Place on the grill pan and cook for 15 minutes.

5.   Make sure to stir the vegetables halfway through

the cooking time.

NUTRITION: Calories: 38; Carbs: 5.8g; Protein:

1.8g; Fat: 1.5g

Air Fried Roasted Summer Squash

Servings: 2

Preparation Time: 5 minutes Cooking Time: 15 minutes

INGREDIENTS

- 1-pound zucchini, sliced into rounds or circles 2 tablespoons extra virgin olive oil
- 1 teaspoon salt
- ½ teaspoon black pepper 1 teaspoon garlic powder

DIRECTIONS

1. Preheat the air fryer at 375OF.

2. Place the grill pan accessory in the air fryer.

3. In a mixing bowl, toss all ingredients until well-combined.

4.　　Place on the grill pan and cook for 15 minutes.

5.　　Stir the vegetables halfway through the cooking time.

NUTRITION: Calories:109; Carbs: 8.6g; Protein: 6.9g; Fat: 6.5g

Grilled Cauliflower Bites

Servings: 1

Cooking Time: 15 minutes

INGREDIENTS

- ½ cups cauliflower florets

- 1 tablespoon olive oil

- 2tablespoons nutritional yeast Salt and pepper to taste

DIRECTIONS

1. Preheat the air fryer at 375oF.

2. Place the grill pan accessory in the air fryer.

3. In a mixing bowl, toss all ingredients until well-combined.

4. Dump the vegetables on to the grill pan and cook for 10 to 15 minutes.

NUTRITION: Calories: 81; Carbs: 6.5g; Protein: 4.2g; Fat: 4.9g

Roasted Air Fried Vegetables

Servings: 4

Cooking Time: 15 minutes

INGREDIENTS

- 12 small red potatoes, scrubbed and halved 1 cup

chopped carrots

- 1 cup butternut squash, peeled and

chopped 1 cup red onion, diced

- 1 red pepper, chopped 1 tablespoon olive oil 1

teaspoon thyme

- 1 teaspoon basil

- 1 teaspoon Italian seasoning

- ½ teaspoon garlic powder Salt and pepper to taste

DIRECTIONS

1. Preheat the air fryer at 375OF.

2. Place the grill pan accessory in the air fryer.

3.　　In a mixing bowl, toss all Ingredients until well-combined.

4.　　Place on the grill pan and cook for 15 minutes.

5.　　Stir the vegetables halfway through the cooking time to grill evenly.

NUTRITION: Calories: 127; Carbs: 22.4g; Protein: 2.6g

Air Fryer Grilled Mexican Corn

Servings: 4

Cooking Time: 15 minutes

INGREDIENTS

- 4 pieces fresh corn on the cob

- ¼ teaspoon chili powder

- ½ teaspoon stone house seasoning

- ¼ cup chopped cilantro 1 lime cut into wedge

- ¼ cup cojita or feta cheese

DIRECTIONS

1. Preheat the air fryer at 375OF.

2. Place the grill pan accessory in the air fryer.

3. Season the corn with chili powder and stone house seasoning.

4. Place on the grill pan and cook for 15 minutes while flipping the corn halfway through the cooking

time.

5.   Serve the corn with cilantro, lime, and feta cheese.

NUTRITION: Calories:102; Carbs: 17g; Protein: 4g; Fat: 3g

Crispy and Spicy Grilled Broccoli in Air Fryer

Servings: 1

Cooking Time: 15 minutes

INGREDIENTS

- 1 head of broccoli, cut into florets

- 2 tablespoons yogurt

- 1 tablespoon chickpea flour

- Salt and pepper to taste

- ½ teaspoon red chili flakes

- 1 tablespoon nutritional yeast

DIRECTIONS

1. Preheat the air fryer at 375OF.

2. Place the grill pan accessory in the air fryer.

3.   Put all Ingredients in a Ziploc bag and shake until well combined.

4.   Dump the ingredients on the grill pan and cook for 15 minutes until crispy.

NUTRITION: Calories: 96; Carbs: 16.9g; Protein: 7.1g; Fat: 1.3g

Lightning Source UK Ltd.
Milton Keynes UK
UKHW020740150621
385538UK00001B/26